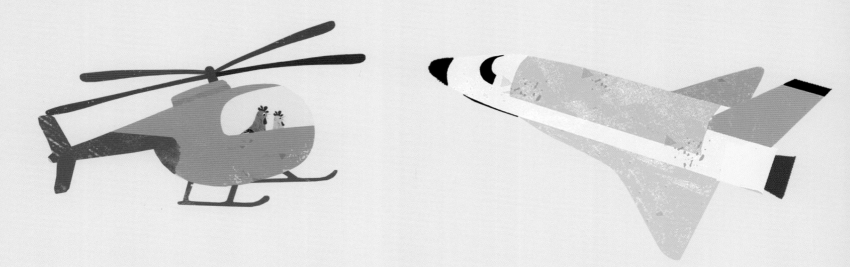

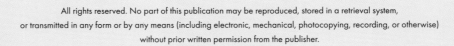

BOXER BOOKS Ltd. and the distinctive Boxer Books logo are trademarks of Union Square & Co., LLC.
Union Square & Co., LLC, is a subsidiary of Sterling Publishing Co., Inc.

Illustrations © 2008 Britta Teckentrup
Text © 2008 Boxer Books Limited

This edition first published in North America in 2023 by Boxer Books Limited.
Originally published as *Big Noisy Book of Busy Vehicles* in 2008.

ISBN 978-1-912757-91-6

Library of Congress Control Number: 2022952453

For information about custom editions, special sales, and premium purchases,
please contact specialsales@unionsquareandco.com.

Printed in China
Lot #:
2 4 6 8 10 9 7 5 3 1
06/23

unionsquareandco.com

Text written by Ronne Randall.
The illustrations were prepared using hand-painted paper and digital collage.

BIG BOOK OF VEHICLES

Illustrated by
Britta Teckentrup

Written by
Ronne Randall

Boxer Books

VEHICLES

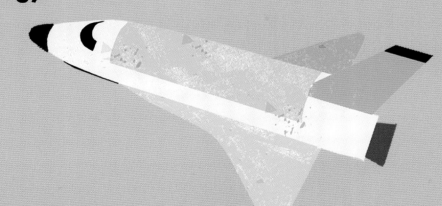

LET'S GET MOVING

We ROLL on wheels

Trams and trains roll on tracks.

Cars and trucks roll along the road.

Tractors have BIG wheels to roll along rough earth.

We FLOAT in the water

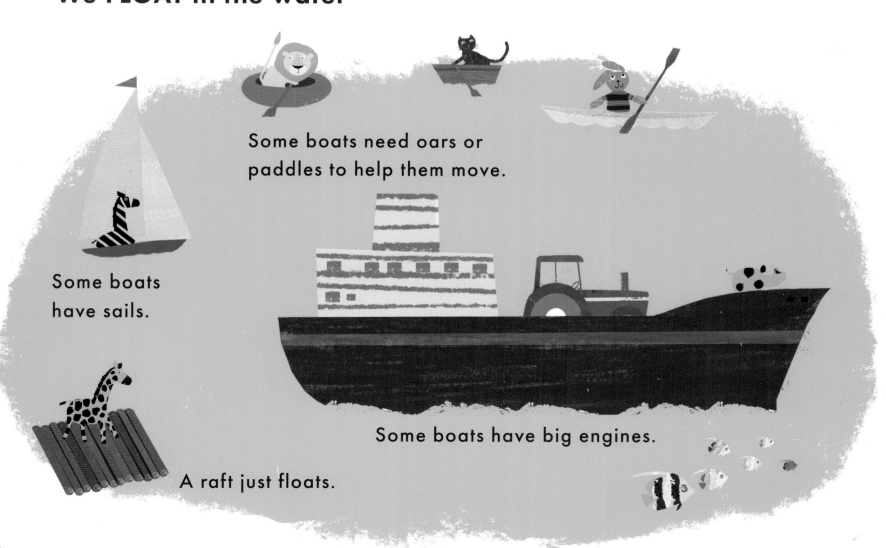

Some boats need oars or paddles to help them move.

Some boats have sails.

Some boats have big engines.

A raft just floats.

We FLY in the air

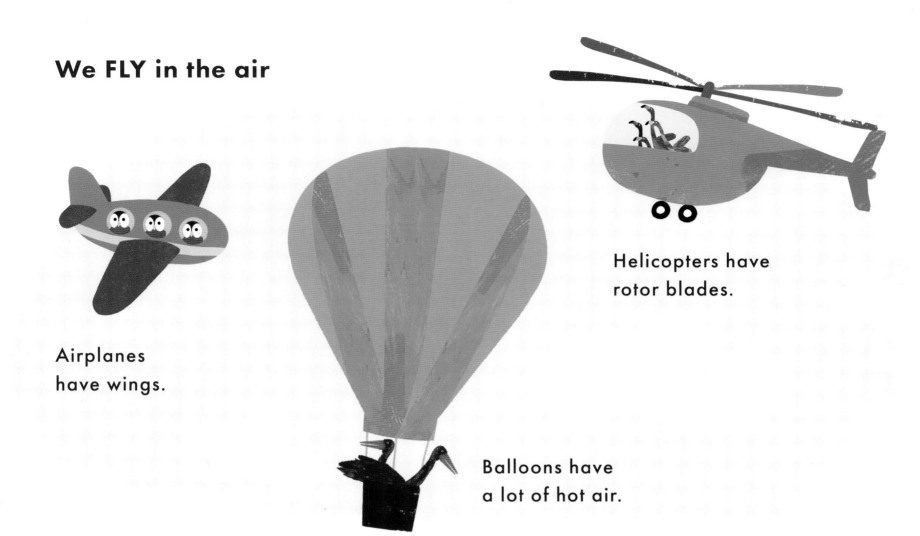

Airplanes
have wings.

Balloons have
a lot of hot air.

Helicopters have
rotor blades.

We SKIM over ice and snow

Snowmobiles have an engine
to zip across the snow.

Dogs help pull a sled.

TIME TO PLAY

All these ways of getting around are good for the environment and for your health.

Bicycles have two wheels.

Tricycles have three wheels.

You can zip around quickly on a scooter.

Fancy flips are fun on a skateboard!

With skates you can
roll along really fast.

You can jump
around on a pogo stick!

You can drive your own toy car,
but watch out for people.

BUSY STREETS
Vehicles are always picking up or delivering.

Some people have their groceries delivered to their home.

Someone has ordered take-out food. This scooter will get it there nice and hot.

The school bus brings children home. They're just in time for ice cream!

Babies travel in strollers.

It's moving day! A big truck arrives
and movers pack the truck with all
the furniture and goods from the home.
A car carries the family to their new home.

Big garbage and recycle trucks come regularly to take
away all your recycling to help our environment.

Busy streets need to stay clean.
The street sweeper sweeps up the litter.

13

IT'S ELECTRIC IN THE CITY

Trams run on tracks with wires overhead.

Electric vehicles are making our world safer and healthier.

Some buses have one level.

Double-decker buses have two levels.

Long tunnels have been made under the ground so trains can run on tracks without getting stuck in traffic in the street.

Underground trains roar through tunnels under the city.

A speedy moped can zip in and out of traffic.

Taxis take you where you want to go.

You can ride in style in a big stretch limo.

Passengers wait for trains on underground platforms.

ON THE HIGHWAY

Tanker trucks can carry all kinds of liquids, from milk to fuel.

Car carriers move cars—lots of them!

Tractor trailors carry great big loads.

Some people take
a motorcycle trip.

Some people take a bus trip.

Some cars pull trailers.

Some people have a vacation home on wheels.

EMERGENCY

Uh-oh! There's been an accident! Don't worry, help is on the way!

The rescue helicopter is on its way.

With flashing lights and sirens, the police are here to help.

If a car is damaged, the tow truck will take it to the garage to be fixed.

If people are hurt, the rescue helicopter will get them to the hospital fast.

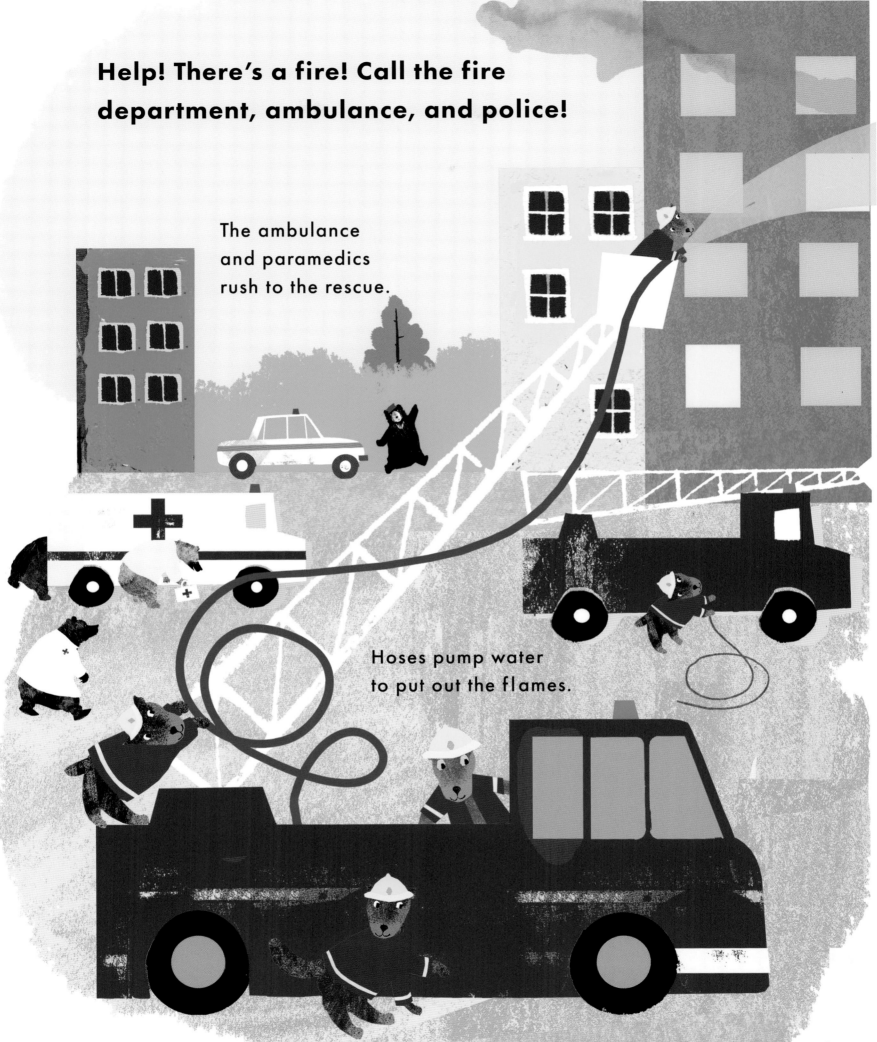

Help! There's a fire! Call the fire department, ambulance, and police!

The ambulance and paramedics rush to the rescue.

Hoses pump water to put out the flames.

Ladders help firefighters climb up high. Fire engines carry everything firefighters need.

BUILDING GOING UP

Schools, homes, and businesses have to be built. This involves lots of people and some huge machines.

Tall cranes lift heavy girders up really high.

Lots of busy machines are working at the building site.

The cement mixer's barrel turns to mix up the cement.

Building site vehicles dig, scoop, and dump.

Bulldozers and diggers dig out lots of soil and rocks.

Dump trucks take away all the rubble, earth, and rocks.

The dump truck drives to a place where it can be emptied.

RIDING THE RAILS

Trains roll on tracks all around the world.

Trains can take you to another town, or another country!

Freight trains carry cabbages and cars, books and bicycles.

Old-fashioned trains moved slowly and used coal and steam to move.

Monorails run on one track.

Passenger trains carry people and their luggage.

A container can carry almost anything.

New high-speed trains go lightning-fast and are much better for the environment.

They move on rails high above the ground.

FUN ON THE FARM

Farms provide our food and some drinks.

The tractor pulls the plow to get the soil ready for planting.

When the grain is tall and ripe, the combine harvester gathers it.

Here's a wagon full of hay. Horses, cows, sheep, and goats will munch on hay all winter.

The pickup truck brings supplies from town to help run this busy farm.

At the dairy, the cows give milk.

The milk tanker carries fresh milk to a processing plant to make sure it is safe to drink.

Some farms only grow vegetables. Vegetarians and vegans prefer not to eat meat or dairy foods. They love vegetables.

SPEED DEMONS

So many speedy vehicles! Which one do you think is fastest?

BMX bikes can go really fast.

Go-karts can go even faster.

Speedboats race across the water.

Racing cars speed around tracks.

Motorcycles can reach amazing speeds.

Supersonic jets boom through the sky,
faster than the speed of sound.

MOUNTAIN HIGH

There are busy vehicles everywhere, even way up in the mountains.

Skiers can take a chairlift to the top of the mountain.

A funicular railway has two cars.

One car goes up while the other car goes down.

Mountain roads are easy for 4x4 vehicles.

You can cross deep valleys in a cable car.

Some people fly off the mountainside in a hang glider. They make sure their harness is buckled in tight, then . . . wheeeeee!

Mountain bikes have thick, strong tires to grip mountain paths.

ALL AT SEA

Oceans are full of busy ships big and small. They sail thousands of miles around the world with passengers and goods.

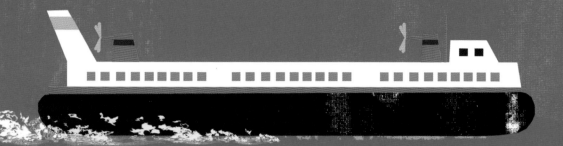

A hovercraft moves on a cushion of air, just above the water.

Ocean liners carry passengers to faraway places. On board are swimming pools, restaurants, and theaters.

Cabin cruisers have engines.

Sailboats move along when the wind fills their sails.

Little tugboats pull big ships, like this red cargo ship, into harbors.

Submarines can travel deep under the sea.

Here comes a fishing boat with today's catch, just in time for dinner!

SNOWY PLACES

**Some places on our planet are cold all year long.
Other places sometimes have snow in winter.**

The snowplow clears a path so that other vehicles can use the road.

Bigger sleds
are pulled by dogs.

Small sleds are great
for zooming down hills.

The Arctic in the north and the Antarctic in the south are
very cold places. We need to make sure that they stay that way.

The icebreaker is powerful enough to break up thick ice so other boats can use the lake.

Snowmobiles don't need a road; they just zip across the snow!

Sleighs are pulled by horses—or sometimes reindeer!

FLYING HIGH

People have flown around the world for many years.
Today, people are looking at ways to make
air travel more friendly for the planet.

Some pilots learn to fly in
two-seater planes with propellers.

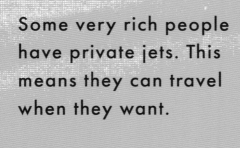

Some very rich people
have private jets. This
means they can travel
when they want.

A helicopter has rotor blades on the roof that turn
very fast and make the helicopter rise into the sky.
Unlike a plane, it does not need a runway.

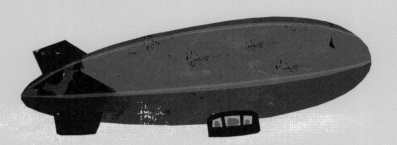

Airships are filled with a gas called helium.
Helium is lighter than air and helps airships to fly.

Hot-air balloons
are filled with
hot air.

Microlights have
very light engines.

Gliders have no engines.
They float on air currents.

The big jumbo jet
will take travelers
to a faraway country.

35

TO THE MOON AND BEYOND

These busy vehicles are out of this world!
Look at what's happening out in space.

The Lunar Module has landed.
The astronauts are off to
explore the moon.

Satellites help send messages
back to Earth. Some send messages,
pictures, and movies to your TV and
smart devices.

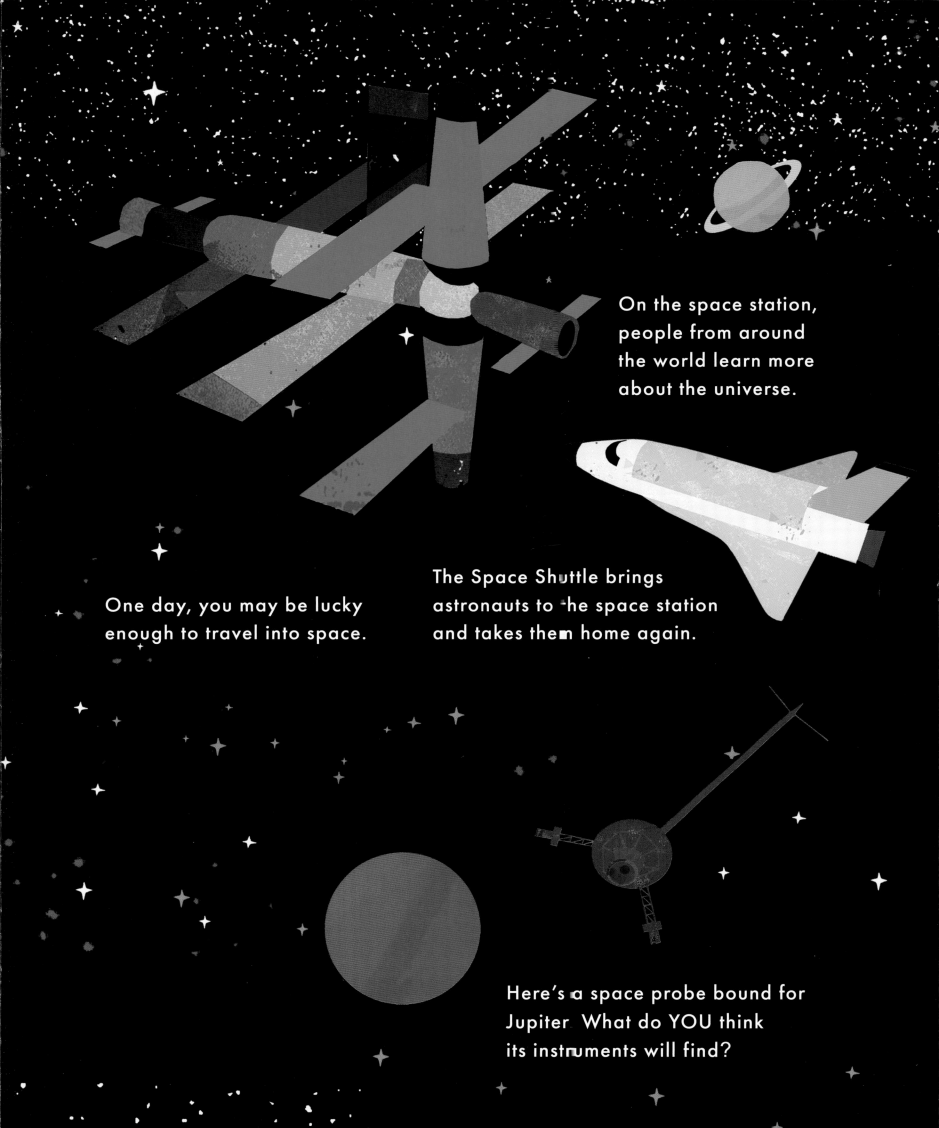

On the space station, people from around the world learn more about the universe.

One day, you may be lucky enough to travel into space.

The Space Shuttle brings astronauts to the space station and takes them home again.

Here's a space probe bound for Jupiter. What do YOU think its instruments will find?